To–

From–

OTHER BOOKS IN THE TO-GIVE-AND-TO-KEEP® SERIES:

Happy Anniversary	To my very Special Husband
Merry Christmas	To my very Special Love
To a very Special Dad	To someone Special in Times of Trouble
To a very Special Daughter	To a very Special Sister
To a very Special Friend	To a very Special Son
To a very Special Granddaughter	To my very Special Wife
To a very Special Grandmother	Welcome to the New Baby
To a very Special Grandpa	Wishing You Happiness

EDITED BY HELEN EXLEY.

Dedicated to Momtom.

Published simultaneously in 1992 by Helen Exley Giftbooks in Great Britain, and Helen Exley Giftbooks LLC, in the USA.

12 11 10

Copyright © Helen Exley 1992
The moral right of the author has been asserted.

ISBN 1-86187-360-3 (Laminate edition)
      1-86187-023-X (Personalised suedel edition)
      1-86187-068-X (Suedel edition)

A copy of the CIP data is available from the British Library on request.
All rights reserved. No part of this publication may be reproduced or transmitted in any form or by any means, electronic or mechanical, including photocopy, recording or any information storage and retrieval system without permission in writing from the Publisher.
Printed in China.

Helen Exley Giftbooks, 16 Chalk Hill, Watford, Herts WD19 4BG, United Kingdom.
Helen Exley Giftbooks LLC, 185 Main Street, Spencer, MA 01562, USA.
www.helenexleygiftbooks.com

'TO A VERY SPECIAL'® AND 'TO-GIVE-AND-TO-KEEP'®
ARE REGISTERED TRADE MARKS OF EXLEY PUBLICATIONS LTD
AND EXLEY GIFTBOOKS.

To a very special®
MOTHER

WRITTEN BY PAM BROWN
ILLUSTRATIONS BY JULIETTE CLARKE

You took all the ordinary things of every
day and made me feel special. Whatever
happens in my life I know, because of you,
that I am worth something.

. . .

A HELEN EXLEY GIFTBOOK

■EXLEY

ONLY A MOTHER

Mothers know when you are
faking.

. . .

Only a mother can send hugs
by post.

. . .

Mothers can do running
repairs actually on the run.

. . .

Only a mother can make Family out of
an assortment of disparate individuals.

. . .

Only a mother can learn to see
through her children's eyes. If she
didn't, she wouldn't stand in a winter
drizzle, clutching a small, sticky paw,
staring at a workman down a hole.

. . .

Mothers are the only people
who tell you the truth when
it's going to hurt.

. . .

Only mothers have lists.
That breed. And grow.

. . .

Mothers are the people who yell after
you waving the things
you've forgotten.

. . .

Mothers are always on stand-by.

. . .

THANK YOU!

Thank you for stocking me up with poems
and tunes to last me all my life. Thank you for
showing me the setting sun for the first time.
And walking with me in the pouring rain.
And scrunching down winter beaches. Thank
you for letting me bring home rocks and
shells and fallen branches. Thank you for
housing my frogs. Thank you for the
excitement of being alive.

. . .

Thank you for "Try hard. Work hard. And if
you can't do it, turn your attention to
something else." Saved a lot of heartache.

. . .

Thanks for never saying, "I told you so."
Well - not often.

Thank you for always being there.

Not intrusively. Not demandingly.

There.

Available at all hours for advice on coughs,

spelling, good books, stains, Mozart, friends'

presents, using libraries, crossword clues.

Et al.

Packed and ready to come if needed.

At once.

Shoulder to cry on.

Someone to tell the news.

Someone to laugh at the Funny.

Someone with an inexhaustible

supply of love.

Whatever I've done.

Always.

. . .

A HAVEN

When I was very small and afraid, you used to put
on the light and show me all the familiar objects in
my room - then flick it off and sit with me in the
darkness until I was quite certain the
shapes were constant.

Dad would insist you close the door behind you,
but you would always sneak a crack of light
into the gloom - just enough to let me see that
nothing stalked my bed.

In a way it's still the same. My anxieties are greater
now, and my world less certain - but you let a little
light into it, so that I can see my problems for
what they are. Things I can deal with - not run from.

. . .

A mother is the person who hears
when you are grizzling silently into
your pillow.

. . .

When it's sorrow beyond keeping,
phone home.

. . .

Love is exciting
But sometimes one needs a quiet
kitchen,
a cup of coffee and one's mother.

. . .

Mothers can dry your tears down a
telephone.

. . .

A mother has the magic glue that
sticks the
broken pieces together.

. . .

WORKING MOTHERS

Take in the laundry. Collect the mended shoes.

Reading tests and driving tests and interviews.

Telephone and train times. P.T.A.

Bacon, cheese and crackers and bunny rabbit hay.

Computers and portfolios, manuscripts and mice.

Transatlantic telex and long-grained rice.

Measle spots and mergers, the ballet school display

And the BBC are asking for an interview *today*.

Till receipts, sea cadets, sandwiches and soap.

Mother - *tell* me, mother - how the *hell* you cope?!

. . .

I am proud of what you do.

I love you for what your are.

Who wants A Totally Domesticated Mother?

This way is so much more exciting!

. . .

I don't know how you fitted me in.

But you did.

And do.

Your life is so full - and yet I know that,

always, always,

There is room for me.

. . .

△ Bricks △

◇ Teddy ◇

⋈ Bear ⋈

Kite

Rag Doll

MEMORIES OF CHILDHOOD

I remember the run home from school, black - stockinged, satchel swinging, the drab day behind me, toast and currant cake ahead. I remember the smell of home - the smell all children hold in their noses, the way puppy dogs do.

I remember you in the kitchen, apron wrapped and waiting for my news.

And now here we are, one old lady and the other one past the middle years, sitting in a tea shop, our carrier bags safely against our ankles, exchanging the news of the week.

Two white heads to any observer, but, for us, two people in disguise. A ghostly shadow of black stockings. A phantom pinafore.

The years have changed us - but brought us closer. Mother and child - friends for life.

. . .

MOTHER LOVE

Mother love is more like tensile
steel than feathers.

Mother love is less meringue than
wholemeal loaf.

Mother love is the fuel that
enables a normal human being to
do the impossible.

Mother love doesn't need
as much sleep
as other sorts.

Mother love doesn't give a damn
about your looks. She thinks
you are beautiful, anyway.

Mother love is the most elastic
thing on earth - but even mother
love can be stretched too far.

Mother love does not come in a
packet, like a Betty Crocker
angel cake. It's a highly
individual business - can
sometimes sink a little in the
middle and sometimes be rather
crisp at the edges.

Mother love is the thing that
makes a mother shake her child
like a rat when he didn't
get run over.

Mother love is like air. It's so
commonplace you don't even
notice it.
Till the supply is cut off.

Mother love is the family's
pilot light.

. . .

WORRY! WORRY! WORRY!

Mothers live in perpetual terror - of fire and flood
and lonely roads, of evil men and lunatic drivers, of
failing brakes and train derailments and aircraft
hitting trees. They only let it show about
three o'clock in the morning.

. . .

Mothers don't really have premonitions. They have
been over every possible eventuality so often - both
good and ill - that whatever happens to you,
they've rehearsed it.

. . .

Hulking great muscle-bound heroes whose mothers have access to their baggage will find extra socks, vitamin C capsules, snipped out articles on the care of the feet and packets of dental floss tucked in among the pitons and ice axes.

. . .

Mothers are inclined to worry. All the time.
Thanks, for not letting it show too much.

. . .

It's all very well saying, "Mum, don't fuss"
- but it is she who discovers you haven't packed your documents.

. . .

STANDING BY ME

I love it when you are excited and pleased
because I've had a success or a stroke of luck.
And I love it all the more when you still think
I'm wonderful when I've fallen flat on my face.

. . .

Thanks for not telling me off in public.
You always got me home
before you let me have it.

. . .

Thanks for not coming all over weepy when I've
been unbelievably stupid.
Thanks for yelling and telling me what a fool
I've been in a variety of well-considered phrases.
And then putting the raging squarely behind us,
and getting down to sorting out
what has to be done.

. . .

Thanks for not giving up on me when I'd been
particularly awful. You were the only
one who didn't.

. . .

I know if I turned up on the doorstep in the
middle of the night, soaked through, with all
my bags and speechless with tears
you'd just say;
"Oh, love. Take off all your clothes.
Put on my big woolly dressing gown."
Let's hope it will never come to that.
But it's nice to know.

. . .

Mother love is the conviction that all her geese
are swans. Which is the only way to keep up
the spirits of kids who are convinced
that they are lame ducks.

. . .

FOR EVERYTHING

Thank you for enduring the unendurable. For making something out of nothing. For giving when your pockets were empty. For loving us when we were totally unlovable. Thank you for doing the impossible with a smile.

(Even if it quivered a little sometimes.)

Thank you for giving me your complete attention
when I explained calculus to you.

. . .

Thank you for earning the money to raise me.
Thank you for meeting me at the school gate.
Thank you for dealing with that Horrible Boy.
Thank you for putting raisins in my lunch bag.
Thank you for explaining Taking Away and
Multiplying.
Thank you for making mumps not too bad at all.
Thank you for always being there when I need you.
And for Surprises.

MOTHERS ACROSS THE WORLD

An engineer has a rapport with the engineers of another country, a mother with half its population.

. . .

Mothers know exactly what life is all about. Not Art. Not Literature. Not Science. All interesting stuff. Worth doing. But basically, basically, it's about children, about people.

You mothers should be the politicians.

. . .

Thank you for making friends with everybody on a day out - ladies in art galleries, bus conductors, shop assistants, old gentlemen feeding the sparrows, old gentlemen living in boxes, lost tourists, ladies on the wrong bus....

Thank you for introducing us to the human race.

. . .

Mums are an interlocking chain that holds the world together.

. . .

FREE TO BE ME

From the very moment I was born, you insisted that
I was myself and not an extension of you and Dad -
that I had not come into existence simply for you to
organize or even to love.

Dear Parents - thank you for giving me the
freedom to love you.

. . .

Thank you for being interested - but never prying.
For being loving - but never drowning me in love.
For building me a nest
- but letting me fly free.

. . .

Thanks for opening all
those doors for me -
but never shoving me
through them.

. . .

Mothers start our lives. They cast on our existence.
They teach us plain and purl.
They give us the basic patterns.
But the good ones - the ones like you - hand over
the needles after a while, and say:
"There's the world, love. Choose yourself some new
shades, some new patterns. Make yourself a life."

. . .

Good mothers give their children
paints and brushes and canvas,
but let them paint
their own picture.

. . .

THANKS TO ALL THE MOTHERS...

...who made hard times seem good times.

...who faked their portions at dinner so that
everyone else got a little more.

...who said go ahead and finish it off - they didn't
fancy ice-cream.

...who persuaded us that living in a dirty downtown
area was exciting.

...who chopped up the best thing in their wardrobe
to make us a party frock overnight.

...who sang us home in the rain.

...who tried their hand at algebra.

...who shared our chickenpox.

...who managed to smile when we ran a fever just
before they were due to go out for
their birthday treat.

...who always found money from the tooth fairy -
even if they had to hunt down the sides of the sofa.

...who only cried a very little when we broke the
best teapot.

...who let us have our own opinions - just as
long as we knew why.

...who let us grow up and fly free.

· · ·